High Blood Pressure
Hypertension

Brought To You by:
GetWell Education

GetWell.org

Contributors:

Lara Moore, Editor

Nicolette F. Asselin, M.D., Consultant

References:

Mayo Clinic

American Heart Association

American Academy of Family Practice

Center for Disease Control

Legal Disclaimers

Manufactured in the United States of America

First Published in 2012

9 7 8 0 6 1 5 7 1 4 6 1 5

Library of Congress Card Number

pending

Copyright © 2012 GetWell Education Foundation

ISBN: 0615714617
ISBN-13: 978-0615714615
E-Book: pending

DEDICATION

We would like to dedicate this booklet to Family and General Practitioners who have seen their roles as physicians changed tremendously in recent years and struggle with inadequate time to care for their patients.

We hope that this booklet assist you in providing the care once possible.

Index

Foreword

Foreword

"There is a staggering amount of information available with web resources today. However, I believe that we need to bring things to a basic level to build better understanding and sounder knowledge."
N. F. Asselin, M.D.

"One way to get high blood pressure is to go mountain climbing over molehills."
Earl Wilson

"Exercise to stimulate, not to annihilate. The world wasn't formed in a day, and neither were we. Set small goals and build upon them."
Lee Haney

Acknowledgments

Thank you to everyone on the board for encouraging this publication.
Thank you to Sherry Roberts, Judy, Sam, Nick, Amy, Sara, and all those involved in the research as well as production.

A word from the Editor

The purpose of this series is to offer health prevention resources for the general public. This series has been constructed to have readers achieve a goal by earning points toward a "Health Certificate.

A word from the Consultant??

In this series readers will learn to understand the source and prevent illnesses. They will understand the basis as well as be able to recognize symptoms. As a physician, I feel that the information available on the web is a great resource but can become quickly overwhelming and discouraging or produce counterproductive fears to readers.

Mission

GetWell Education mission's:

Is to offer a basic knowledge on topics that may have a positive effect on their lives.

To prevent unnecessary medical costs and assists people in leading healthier lives.

To empower readers to become an active participant in their care.

To inspire self-respect and knowledge to contribute to reduce health care cost.

To achieve these goals, the team dedicated to this Health Series, is committed to providing quality education, encompassing individual differences in education and personal background.

The aim of this series is to share information that will encourage self-respect and a sense of dignity rather than anxiety or avoidance of health issues.

Hypertension

Chapter 1 Introduction

It may be harmful to your health not to know about this topic! On the other hand, you may already know what we are about to share with you.

Before you read this book

1. Take the Quiz on the back of this booklet. If you score a 100% move to level 2 series. If you score less than that, read the booklet and take the quiz again when you are done.

2. It is important that you choose a time when you can relax so you can retain the important facts you are about to read. Presently, we are so bombarded with information that it is, at time, difficult to remember simple things. Less is better.

3. This booklet is to represent the building blocks on which you will construct important life changing behaviors as well as learn to recognize life-changing information.

Name:

_____

Date: _____/ _____/ _____

Assessment

Score before reading: _____

Score after reading: _____

Notes:

Chapter 2 Definition

What is High Blood Pressure?

Blood pressure is the measurement of fluid pressure applied to arterial walls.

High blood pressure, also called hypertension is a common condition in which the force of the blood against your artery walls is high enough that it may eventually cause health problems, such as heart disease and stroke.

Common sense comparison*: Think of your home's plumbing system or simply your tires..*

How is it determined?

Blood pressure is determined by the amount of blood your heart pumps and the amount of resistance in your arteries.

> ➢ You can have hypertension (high blood pressure) for years without symptoms.

Common sense comparison*: If water pumped by your well or city water became too high, eventually* *the pipes in your home would give in. Likewise if the pipes were blocked or over filled, it may cause backpressure and the plumbing in your home may start giving up. However, you may not see the damage for a long time.*

What are the risks?

Uncontrolled hypertension increases your risk of serious health problems, including heart diseases, stroke, aneurysm etc..

How does it do that?

It damages and scars your arteries, including those of your heart and your brain.

Common sense example: *Think of a pregnant women and what her belly looks like after the birth of her child.*

Blood pressure normally rises and falls throughout the day, but it can cause health problems if it stays high for a long time. Having high blood pressure raises your risk for heart disease and stroke, leading causes of death in the United States.[1]

Summary:

High blood pressure is called "silent killer" because many people don't realize they have it.

Reference

1) Miniño AM, Murphy SL, Xu J, et al. Deaths: Final data for 2008. National Vital Statistics Reports; vol 59 no 10. Hyattsville, MD: National Center for Health Statistics. 2011.

Hypertension

Chapter 3 Symptoms

How do I know I have high blood pressure (HBP)?

The best advocate for your health is you.

Having your blood pressure checked on a regular basis is important. Most pharmacies, these days, have a special station for that purpose.

Important:

High blood pressure often has no warning signs or symptoms.

HBP is largely a symptomless condition.

If you ignore your blood pressure because you think symptoms will alert you to the problem, you are taking a dangerous chance with your life. Everybody needs to know his or her blood pressure numbers, and everyone needs to prevent high blood pressure from developing.

There's a common misconception that people with high blood pressure, also called hypertension, will experience symptoms such as nervousness, sweating, difficulty sleeping or facial flushing.

Hypertensive crisis

Hypertensive crisis is an emergency. Obvious symptoms may occur, only when blood-pressure readings soar to dangerously high levels (systolic of 180 or higher or diastolic of 110 or higher). Blood pressure, in these ranges is known as hypertensive crisis, and **emergency medical treatment is needed.**

> ➢ Severe headaches
> ➢ Severe anxiety
> ➢ Shortness of breath
> ➢ Nosebleeds

Hypertensive crisis is an emergency. The consequences of uncontrolled blood pressure in this range can be severe and include:

○ Stroke
○ Loss of consciousness
○ Memory loss
○ Heart attack
○ Damage to the eyes and kidneys

- o Loss of kidney function
- o Aortic dissection
- o Angina (unstable chest pain)
- o Pulmonary edema (fluid backup in the lungs)
- o Eclampsia (causes coma or seizures in pregnant women)

Headache

Symptoms of headache are very serious as they indicate a much more serious stage of HBP called **Hypertensive crisis**. These symptoms should not be ignored and <u>immediate medical attention</u> should be obtained. If your doctor cannot take you in go to an emergency room.

The headache may be so bad that you or the person afflicted with the headache may not want to seek medical attention. As last resort, call 9-1-1.

➢ If access to medical care is not possible immediately, the use of **ice**, **lying down** and **complete rest** may help.

➢ If the headache stops, **do** seek medical attention

as soon as it is made available. It is important to address the cause of the crisis and use preventive measure for the future.

Reference

1) American Heart Association

Chapter 4 The cause

What is the Cause of Primary High Blood Pressure?

Causes unknown

In 90-95% of cases the cause is unknown. In fact, you can have high blood pressure for years without knowing it. That is why it is referrer to a "silent killer" – it creeps up on you. The most common cause of secondary hypertension is due to kidney disease.

Just because doctors only rarely know what causes primary high blood pressure, does not mean you cannot influence it.

You have the power to reduce your risk for stroke, heart and kidney diseases. These steps are discussed in this next section discussing your risks, such as conditions and behaviors.

Your Risks

Conditions:

Diabetes, kidney and heart disease, atherosclerosis (disease of arteries), sleep apnea are examples.

Behavior:

Healthy behaviors contribute to keeping your blood pressure low, which in turn decreases your risk of heart disease.

Diet

Sodium is the element in salt that can raise blood pressure. Most of the sodium we eat comes from processed and restaurant foods. Eating too much sodium can increase blood pressure. [7]

Daily recommended: 1,500 mg.

Common sense example: ¼ tsp is 2000 milligrams

Not eating enough potassium (from fruits and vegetables) can also increase blood pressure. Potassium has the ability to lessen the effect of sodium. [7]

Daily recommended: 4,700 mg.

Weight

Being overweight can cause high blood pressure.

Physical Inactivity

Not getting enough exercise can make you gain weight, which can lead to high blood pressure.

Daily: 30-60 minutes of physical activity

Alcohol Use

Drinking too much alcohol can raise your blood pressure. [7]

Maximum daily: 8 ounces of wine for men and four ounces of wine for women.

Tobacco Use

Smoking raises your risk for high blood pressure. [7]

Medications

Certain drugs, such as amphetamines (stimulants), diet pills, and some medications used for cold and allergy symptoms such as pseudoephedrine, tend to raise blood pressure.

Genetics:

The rate of high blood pressure in African American in the United States is among the highest in the world. It also appears to occur at an earlier age and consequently and are at higher risk for heart attack, stroke, heart failure and kidney complications from high blood pressure.

Risk factors for heart diseased and stroke amplify one another rather than just adding up. The more risk factors you have, the higher your risk for heart disease and stroke.

If these life style changes don't get your blood pressure down to normal level, your doctor may prescribe a blood pressure lowering medication.

Prehypertension

Blood pressure levels that are higher than normal put you at risk for developing high blood pressure.

Chapter 5
Measurements

How is hypertension measured?

There are two forces at play:

Systolic: The first occurs as bloods pumps out of the heart into the arteries to give oxygen to your body.

Diastolic: The second occurs when your heart rests between heartbeats.

Common sense example:

Unlike the pressure in your tires, the body has two numbers. Since there are two pressures: the force of the heart and the resistance of arteries.

Blood pressure readings

These two forces are represented in a blood pressure reading.

S/D or Systolic/Diastolic

Example = 120/78 mm Hg

Lower than 120/80 mm Hg is the most desirable reading in this list. The American Heart Association recommends this as optimal.

120-139/80-89 is considered pre-hypertension in this range.

Systolic blood pressure of 140 or higher is considered high and should be evaluated by a physician immediately. If your blood pressure is 140/90 or higher, you are at risk for stroke, heart attack and other complication.

Your health is your responsibility, so make sure you know your numbers and take control to manage your risk factors for heart disease and stroke.

What are your numbers?

- ➢ Blood pressure

- ➢ Cholesterol

- ➢ Weight

Notes:

- ➢ My blood pressure: _____

- ➢ My cholesterol:_____

- ➢ My weight:_____

Hypertension

Chapter 6 Problems

What problems can it cause?

It is important to remember that you may have high blood pressure for a long time before you develop continuous symptoms.

Damage caused by a stroke

Strokes can happen in a number of ways.

Ischemic stroke:

An ischemic stroke is caused by a complete arterial blockage and depravation of oxygen to tan area of the brain. Fig. 1

Hemorrhagic stroke:

Hemorrhagic stroke is caused by a weakness and rupture in the vessel. It causes bleeding in an area of the brain. Fig..2

Brain Stroke

Ischemic Stroke   *Hemorrhagic Stroke*

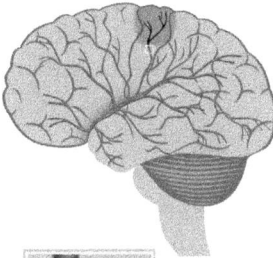

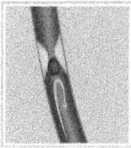

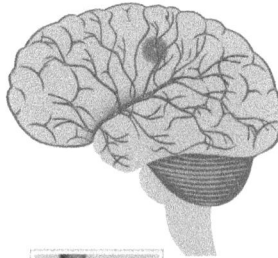

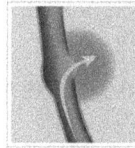

Blockage of blood vessels; lack of blood flow to affected area   Rupture of blood vessels; leakage of blood

Figure 1   Figure 2

How do I know whether I had a stroke?

Strokes can be minor and unnoticeable. The reason for that is that it may be small or affect an area that is not perceivable in your day to day living.

On the other hand, it is very obvious, if it affects a larger vessel and for example, a motor function. In such case one side of your body is unable to move.

Symptoms such as:

- o Sudden numbness or weakness of the face, arm or leg, especially on one side of the body.

- o Sudden confusion, trouble speaking or understanding.

- o Sudden trouble seeing in one or both eyes

- o Sudden trouble walking, dizziness, loss of balance or coordination.

- o Sudden, severe headache with no know cause.

Any or all of these symptoms are warning signs of a stroke and not to be taken lightly. If you or someone around you is having these symptoms, **call 9-1-1 immediately**.

Why is time so important?

Today new medications may stop strokes and heart attacks in progress and reduce the impact of the damage., However, to be effective, these drugs must be given relatively quickly after symptoms first appear. So don't delay – get help immediately if you or someone is having these symptoms.

Stroke and heart attack are life and death emergencies-**every seconds counts**.

Not all these signs occur in every stroke. Sometimes they go away and return. If any occur, get help fast!

Chapter 7 Treatments

How does one treat hypertension?

1. Lifestyle changes and behavior
2. Medications

First line of treatment is behavior modification, life style changes and addressing conditions such as diabetes and high cholesterol.

Second line is blood pressure medication.

Both are treatments that need to be maintained daily not just under certain "conditions".

High blood pressure is a lifelong disease. It can be controlled but is not curable. If your doctor has prescribed medication for you, take it exactly as prescribed for as long as the doctor tells you to take it. Decreasing dosage or not taking the medication at all is dangerous.

If you change the dose or go off the medication, it won't be effective and your blood pressure will rise, putting you at risk for heart attack, stroke, heart and kidney failure.

Medication should be combined with lifestyle changes such as eating low-saturated-fat, low-salt diet, maintaining a healthy weight, getting plenty of physical activity (30-60 minutes daily), sufficient rest at night and not using tobacco products.

Lifestyle changes

After all medical conditions have been addressed and or eliminated, the following should also be considered.

Diet

Salt (sodium) 1500 mg/day

Salt is not all bad, it is good but in moderation. Life without salt would be dreadful! I am sure you will agree.

Only in extreme circumstances should you be subjected to a no salt diet. Children especially need a balance diet.

Some people are more "salt sensitive" than others, so eating salty foods adds to their high blood pressure. Salt holds excess fluid in your body and can put an added burden on your heart. However, in some countries with extreme heat salt is an important part of a diet as it helps people retain needed fluid to avoid dehydration..

It is important to pay attention to your salt intake as sodium is contained in a lot of prepared food. (canned food, baking soda, cheese, dried fruits and even medications).

Fat

Fats are not all bad, they are important.

What is good fat? Any fat derived from vegetable source and fish, rather than animal fats,. Example: Olive oil.

These are called unsaturated fats. They do not increase the total cholesterol.

Weight

If you have tried a number of ways to loose weight but have not achieved your desired weight, don't go at it alone. There are many programs out there that may be fun and rewarding. Life style changes are not simple, but have the potential to change your life forever.

Smoking

If you have tried a number of ways to stop smoking but have not been able to stop, don't go at it alone. There is a true physical addiction to address as well as simple psychological reasons that keeps you from being able to stop.

Quitting does not need to be painful. There are many programs out there that may be fun and rewarding. Life style changes are not simple, but have the potential to change your life forever. On the other hand, recurrent failures are not a positive reinforcement and become a reason to stop trying.

Medical conditions

Again, any medical conditions, that may affect your blood pressure, need the highest priority. Otherwise, any other efforts may be fruitless.

Example, if you have a medical condition that cause you to retain fluid, or a heart or kidney condition, no lifestyle changes can address the primary medical condition.

Medical Treatment

There are a variety of prescription drugs available for this condition. Your doctor will need to decide what works best for you.

Examples of these medicines are:

- o Diuretics, more commonly called water pills, reduce water retention.
- o Beta-Blocker-reduces heart rate.
- o Calcium Channel Blocker-that act on the muscle of your heart and vessels.
- o ACE inhibitors: Inhibits a certain chemical called Angiotensin II.
- o Blocker of Central Sympathetic System: Help relax vessels.

If you have already seen your doctor and he has prescribed a medication, finish this booklet and go to the level 2 booklets, where these drugs are discussed in more details.

How do I know that these medications will not do me more harm than good?

It is important to keep a dialogue with your physician.   Certain medicines do not work for everyone. Since there are many options, your patience is very valuable for a successful treatment. In time, you will find, with your physician, the best and most effective treatment.

www.ingramcontent.com/pod-product-compliance
Lightning Source LLC
Chambersburg PA
CBHW060545030426
42337CB00021B/4438